UNVEILING

FLORENCE

Your Travel Guide to The Cradle of The Renaissance

ESSENTIALS EDITION

ITALY UNCOVERED SEARIES

Presented by

GUIDES

Discover Your Journey

West Agora Int

a WEST AGORA INT S.R.L. Brand
www.tailoredtravelguides.com
Edited by WEST AGORA INT S.R.L.
WEST AGORA INT S.R.L. All Rights Reserved
Copyright © WEST AGORA INT S.R.L., 2023

WIKI

Florence: The Cradle of the Renaissance and a Beacon of Artistic Heritage

Florence, the capital city of Italy's Tuscany region, is a city that resonates with the echoes of the Renaissance, a period that fundamentally shaped the course of Western art and culture. Founded by Julius Caesar in 59 BC as a settlement for his veteran soldiers, Florence rose to prominence in the medieval period, particularly the 14th to 16th centuries, as a center of trade, finance, and, most importantly, art and culture.

The city's historical significance is deeply intertwined with the rise of the Medici family, who were instrumental in fostering the Renaissance movement. Their patronage of the arts led to the creation of some of the most iconic works in history. Florence's streets, squares, and buildings are living museums, showcasing the genius of artists like Michelangelo, Leonardo da Vinci, and Botticelli.

Florence is not just a testament to its glorious past; it is a city that continues to celebrate and preserve its rich artistic heritage. The Uffizi Gallery and the Accademia Gallery house some of the most important collections of Renaissance art in the world, including Michelangelo's David and Botticelli's The Birth of Venus. The city's architecture, characterized by landmarks like the Florence Cathedral with its magnificent dome engineered by Brunelleschi and the historic Ponte Vecchio bridge, stands as a testament to the ingenuity and artistic vision of the Renaissance architects.

The city's culinary scene reflects its rich cultural heritage, offering a blend of traditional Tuscan cuisine with modern Italian gastronomy. Florence's markets and restaurants are a delight for food enthusiasts, offering local specialties like ribollita and bistecca alla fiorentina.

WIKI

Florence's commitment to preserving its cultural and architectural heritage is evident in its meticulous care of historic sites and its regulations to protect its artistic legacy. The city faces the challenge of balancing the preservation of its historical sites with the demands of modern urban life and tourism.

Florence has been home to several notable figures, not only in the arts but also in science and political thought, including Dante Alighieri, Galileo Galilei, and Niccolò Machiavelli. The city's intellectual and artistic influence extended well beyond its borders, shaping the course of Western civilization.

Today, Florence stands as a beacon of art, history, and culture. It is a city that offers a journey through time, where every street, building, and artwork tells the story of a pivotal era in human history. For those seeking to immerse themselves in the legacy of the Renaissance and the beauty of Italian art and culture, Florence offers an unparalleled experience.

CONTENTS

- 1 — GREETINGS AND RECOMMENDATIONS FROM LOCALS
- 3 — PRACTICAL INFORMATION
- 10 — TOP ATTRACTIONS IN FLORENCE
- 22 — HIDDEN GEMS AND LESSER-KNOWN SIGHTS IN FLORENCE
- 31 — PARKS AND GARDENS IN FLORENCE
- 35 — FLORENCE'S CULINARY SCENE
- 40 — SHOPPING IN FLORENCE
- 43 — FAMILY-FRIENDLY ACTIVITIES IN FLORENCE
- 46 — FLORENCE BY NIGHT
- 58 — ART AND CULTURE IN FLORENCE
- 62 — HISTORICAL AND ARCHITECTURAL LANDMARKS IN FLORENCE
- 66 — DAY TRIPS FROM FLORENCE
- 71 — END NOTE

FLORENCE

THE CRADLE OF THE RENAISSANCE

Nestled in the lush heart of Tuscany, Florence, or 'Firenze' in Italian, stands as an emblem of the Renaissance's grandeur, an unforgettable city that intertwines rich cultural history with an enduring artistic legacy. It is a place where every street, piazza, and building seems to tell a story, resonating deeply with those who walk its ancient paths. From the majestic Duomo, crowned by Brunelleschi's awe-inspiring dome, to the historic Ponte Vecchio bridge, Florence is a city where art and architecture are not just attractions but the very fabric of life.

As you wander through the city, the Florence Cathedral, with its intricate marble façade, will leave you breathless, while the Uffizi Gallery, housing masterpieces by Botticelli, Michelangelo, and Leonardo da Vinci, offers a journey through the pinnacle of Renaissance art. Yet, the charm of Florence extends beyond its famous landmarks. The city's numerous squares, including the lively Piazza della Signoria, buzz with the energy of daily Florentine life, hosting vibrant markets and cozy cafés that invite lingering over a cappuccino or a glass of Chianti.

Florence's culinary landscape is as rich as its art. From bustling trattorias serving hearty Tuscan fare to Michelin-starred establishments offering innovative cuisine, the city is a paradise for food lovers. Indulge in traditional dishes like ribollita and bistecca alla fiorentina, and savor gelato as you stroll along the Arno River at sunset. This is a city that engages all the senses, where every meal is a celebration of history and flavor.

Beyond the city, the Tuscan countryside beckons with its rolling hills, olive groves, and vineyards. A short journey can lead you to charming towns like Fiesole, with its stunning views of Florence, or the renowned vineyards of the Chianti region, where the art of winemaking has been perfected over centuries.

This comprehensive travel guide is meticulously crafted to be your window into the soul of Florence. It encompasses everything from the city's top attractions and hidden gems to the finest places for dining, shopping, and experiencing local culture. Each section of the guide is infused with detailed insights, practical tips, and expert recommendations, ensuring that your journey through Florence is as enriching as it is enchanting. Whether it's your first visit or your fiftieth, Florence is a city that never ceases to amaze, a place where each corner holds a new discovery, and every visit feels like coming home. Let this guide be your companion as you explore the timeless beauty and endless mysteries of Florence.

GREETINGS AND INSIGHTS FROM LOCALS

Benvenuto, dear traveler! Welcome to Florence, the cradle of the Renaissance, where every cobblestone, piazza, and palazzo whispers tales of artistic grandeur and historical intrigue. As a true Fiorentino, I've meandered through our city's age-old streets and basked in the glow of its cultural richness, and I'm eager to guide you to the cherished experiences and hidden gems known only to a true local.

Embark on your Florentine adventure by immersing yourself in our storied customs. A warm "buongiorno" and a genuine smile can open the doors to the city's heart, as you wander through the shadow of Brunelleschi's dome, along the Arno's banks, and through the vibrant markets and artisan workshops that are the lifeblood of our city.

You might find yourself captivated by the allure of the Uffizi Gallery. Here, the masterpieces of Botticelli, Michelangelo, and Da Vinci are not mere artworks but portals to an era where Florence was the epicenter of artistic innovation and philosophical thought.

For a taste of our culinary heritage, venture to the bustling Mercato Centrale. Here, under its iron-and-glass canopy, you can savor the flavors of Tuscany, from a hearty ribollita to a slice of luscious cantucci accompanied by a glass of Vin Santo.

When the spirit of exploration calls, ascend to Piazzale Michelangelo. The panoramic views from this beloved spot are a breathtaking spectacle of Florence's terracotta rooftops, majestic Duomo, and the rolling Tuscan hills beyond – a vista that captures the essence of the city's timeless beauty.

As twilight descends, the historic Ponte Vecchio beckons. This ancient bridge, with its glittering jewelry shops and the soft glow of streetlights, creates a magical atmosphere, perfect for a moment of reflection or a romantic stroll.

In the heart of the city, the Florence Cathedral (Il Duomo) stands as a testament to human ingenuity and artistic skill. Its intricate facade and the soaring dome are symbols of Florence's enduring influence on art and architecture.

Florence's true charm lies in its seamless blend of art, history, and the vibrant daily life of its people. We, the Fiorentini, are here with open hearts, ready to share the splendor of our city with you. Arrivederci, dear traveler, and may your journey through Florence be filled with awe-inspiring discoveries and the joy of the Tuscan spirit!

PRACTICAL INFORMATION

Currency	The currency used in Florence, like the rest of Italy, is the Euro (€). It's advisable to have some cash for smaller shops or markets, although credit cards are widely accepted.

Transportation	Florence's compact city center is best explored on foot. For longer distances, the city offers an efficient public transportation system, including buses and a tramline. Taxis are readily available, and bike rentals are a popular choice for a leisurely tour of the city.

Driving in Florence	Driving in Florence can be challenging due to limited parking, ZTL (Limited Traffic Zones), and heavy traffic. It's recommended to use public transport or park outside the city center.

Climate	Florence enjoys a humid subtropical climate. Summers are hot and dry, while winters are cool and damp. The best times to visit are spring (April to June) and fall (September to October) for pleasant temperatures and fewer tourists.

Language	Italian is the official language. English is widely spoken in tourist areas, but learning a few Italian phrases will enhance your experience.

PRACTICAL INFORMATION

Power sockets and adapters   Italy uses Type C, F, and L plugs, and the standard voltage is 230V. Travelers from outside Europe will likely need a power adapter.

Shopping   Florence is famous for its leather goods, artisanal crafts, jewelry, and fashion. Shops usually open from 9:30 am to 7:30 pm but may close for a siesta in the afternoon.

Tipping   Tipping is not compulsory in Italy, but it is appreciated for exceptional service. In restaurants, a service charge might already be included in the bill.

PRACTICAL INFORMATION

USEFUL LINKS AND PHONE NUMBERS

Emergency Services
All Emergencies: 112
Police: 113
Fire Brigade: 115
Medical Emergencies: 118

Transportation
Florence Airport: +39 055 30615, www.aeroporto.firenze.it/en/
ATAF (Local Bus Service): +39 800 424500.
www.fsbusitalia.it/content/fsbusitalia/it/toscana.html
Trenitalia (National Railway): +39 06 68475475,
www.trenitalia.com/en.html

Tourist Information
Official Tourism Site of Tuscany,
www.visittuscany.com/en/index.html
Official Tourism Site of Florence: www.feelflorence.it/en
Florence card: www.firenzecard.it/en

Hospitals
Careggi Hospital: +39 055 794111, www.aou-careggi.toscana.it/internet/index.php?lang=en

Local Government
Municipality of Florence: +39 055 055, https://en.comune.fi.it/ & www.comune.fi.it

Maps
For print versions - quick acces through QR codes after the End Note

Florence maps: www.ontheworldmap.com/italy/city/florence/
Florence General Map:
www.ontheworldmap.com/italy/city/florence/large-detailed-map-of-florence.jpg
Florence Tourist Map:
www.ontheworldmap.com/italy/city/florence/florence-tourist-map.jpg
Florence City Center Map:
www.ontheworldmap.com/italy/city/florence/florence-city-centre-map.jpg
Florence Travel Map:
www.ontheworldmap.com/italy/city/florence/florence-travel-map.jpg
Florence Public Transport Map:
www.feelflorence.it/sites/www.feelflorence.it/files/2022-09/Mappa%20Bus%20Firenze.pdf
Florence Bike Map:
www.feelflorence.it/sites/www.feelflorence.it/files/2023-11/BIKE%20MAP.pdf
Region Tourist Routes:
www.feelflorence.it/sites/www.feelflorence.it/files/2023-04/Mappa_Cammini%20Area%20Fiorentina_ENG_DIGITALE.pdf

PRACTICAL INFORMATION
FLORENCE AND SURROUNDINGS

Free high resolution & download at: https://osm.org/go/xX66oPd Copyright @ OpenStreetMaps

PRACTICAL INFORMATION
FLORENCE AND SURROUNDINGS

Free high resolution & download at: https://osm.org/go/xX66oPd Copyright @ OpenStreetMaps

FLORENCE CITY CENTER MAP

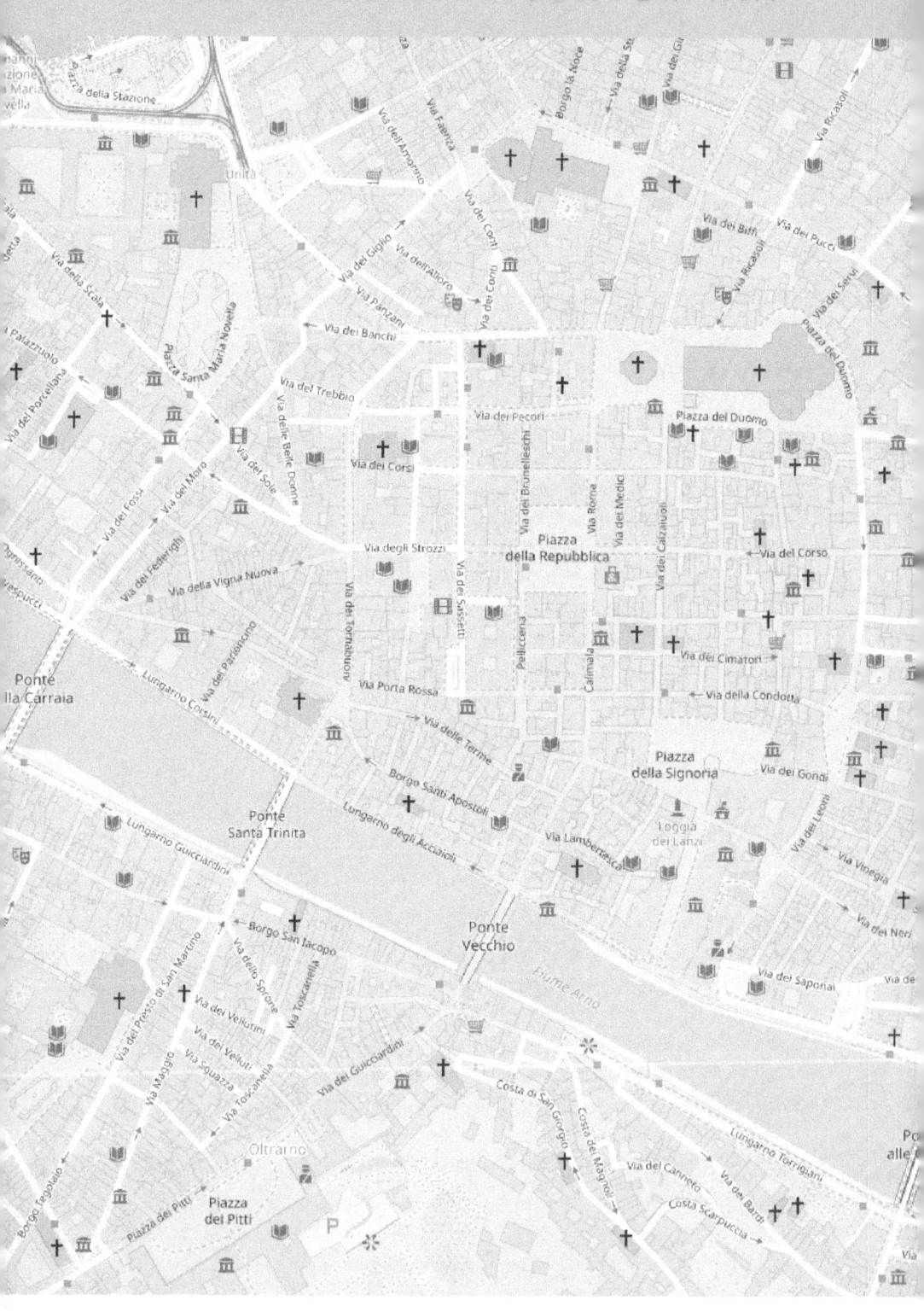

Free high resolution & download at: https://osm.org/go/xdQQAs3O Copyright @ OpenStreetMaps

FLORENCE CITY CENTER MAP

TOP ATTRACTIONS IN FLORENCE

FLORENCE CATHEDRAL

The Florence Cathedral, an architectural masterpiece, stands as a testament to the ingenuity of the Renaissance. Known locally as the Duomo, its most striking feature is Brunelleschi's majestic red dome, a marvel of engineering that dominates the Florence skyline. The cathedral's exterior, a symphony of colored marbles, creates a stunning visual impact. Inside, the vast space is adorned with intricate frescoes and stained glass windows, each telling a story from a bygone era. The highlight for many is the opportunity to climb the dome itself, a challenging ascent that rewards climbers with a panoramic view of the city, revealing Florence in all its historical and architectural glory.

Tip: To fully appreciate the cathedral, consider visiting early in the morning or late in the afternoon to avoid the crowds. The climb to the dome involves narrow, steep stairs, so it's advisable for visitors to be in good physical condition. Booking in advance can save you time waiting in line.

Location: Piazza del Duomo, 50122 Firenze FI, Italy.

Website: www.ilgrandemuseodelduomo.it

UFFIZI GALLERY

The Uffizi Gallery, a cornerstone of Florence's artistic heritage, is a world-renowned art museum that stands as a testament to the city's significant contributions to the Renaissance. Within its walls, visitors are enveloped in the depth and beauty of masterpieces by the greatest artists of the era. The gallery's vast collection includes Botticelli's ethereal "The Birth of Venus" and "Primavera," Michelangelo's profound works, and the ingenious creations of Leonardo da Vinci. Each corridor and room within the Uffizi unfolds like a storied tapestry, rich with history and artistic splendor. The architecture of the gallery itself, characterized by elongated corridors and grandiose rooms, enhances the immersive experience, making it a place where art history truly comes to life. The Uffizi is not just a gallery; it's a journey through the pinnacle of human creativity and an essential experience for anyone seeking to understand the essence of the Renaissance.

Tip: To fully appreciate the gallery, consider allocating several hours or even a full day for your visit. The collection is extensive, and there is much to see and absorb. For those with limited time, focusing on the must-see artworks may be more feasible.

Location: Piazzale degli Uffizi, 6, 50122 Firenze FI, Italy
Website: www.uffizi.it/en/the-uffizi

PONTE VECCHIO

Ponte Vecchio, an iconic symbol of Florence, is more than a mere crossing over the Arno River; it's a historic monument that captures the essence of the city's rich past. Renowned for being the only Florentine bridge to survive World War II, this medieval stone bridge is famed for its rows of jewelry shops, a tradition dating back to the time of the Medici. As you walk through these time-honored shops, you're walking in the footsteps of centuries of history. By day, the bridge buzzes with activity, with locals and tourists alike admiring its craftsmanship and browsing its glittering displays. At night, Ponte Vecchio transforms, with its soft lights reflecting off the river, creating a romantic and enchanting atmosphere that makes for a perfect evening stroll. The bridge not only offers a unique shopping experience but also stunning views of the river and the city, making it a must-visit landmark for anyone exploring Florence.

Tip: To capture the true beauty of Ponte Vecchio, consider visiting at both day and night. The views from the bridge are spectacular at sunset. For photographers, capturing the bridge from various angles, including from the nearby bridges, can yield stunning images.

Location: Ponte Vecchio, 50125 Firenze FI, Italy
Website: www.feelflorence.it/en/node/12057

PALAZZO VECCHIO

Palazzo Vecchio stands as a monumental emblem of Florence's storied past, serving as the city's town hall and a beacon of its rich political and cultural history. This formidable fortress-like palace, overlooking the Piazza della Signoria, is an architectural marvel, showcasing the splendor of Renaissance art and design. Inside, visitors are greeted with lavishly decorated chambers and courtyards, adorned with artworks by celebrated artists like Michelangelo and Vasari. The Salone dei Cinquecento, the palace's most grandiose hall, is famed for its expansive size and stunning frescoes, depicting pivotal moments in Florence's history. Climbing the Arnolfo Tower, part of the palace, rewards visitors with panoramic views of Florence, offering a unique perspective of the city's red rooftops and bustling squares. Palazzo Vecchio is not just a historical site; it's a journey through the ages, where every room tells a story of power, intrigue, and artistic genius.

Tip: To enhance your visit, consider joining one of the guided tours which provide fascinating insights into the palace's history and its role in Florentine life. Also, the evening offers a more tranquil atmosphere to explore the palace's treasures.

Location: P.za della Signoria, 50122 Firenze FI, Italy
Website: www.florence-museum.com/palazzo-vecchio.php

GALLERIA DELL'ACCADEMIA

The Galleria dell'Accademia in Florence is a sanctuary of Renaissance art, most renowned for being the home of Michelangelo's magnificent sculpture, "David." This awe-inspiring masterpiece stands at the heart of the gallery, a symbol of beauty and strength, captivating visitors from around the world. Beyond "David," the gallery houses a remarkable collection of Renaissance paintings, sculptures, and a rare assembly of musical instruments, offering a comprehensive glimpse into the artistic revolution of the period. Each hall and corridor in the Galleria dell'Accademia tells a story of artistic innovation and brilliance, making it an essential visit for art enthusiasts. While smaller in size compared to the vast Uffizi Gallery, the Accademia offers a more focused and intimate experience, allowing visitors to immerse themselves fully in the works of Michelangelo and his contemporaries. The gallery's collection extends beyond Michelangelo, featuring works by artists such as Botticelli and Ghirlandaio, each contributing to the rich tapestry of Renaissance art.

Tip: The Galleria dell'Accademia is one of Florence's most popular tourist destinations, so booking tickets in advance is highly recommended to avoid long waiting times. Opting for an early morning or late afternoon visit can also provide a more peaceful viewing experience.

Location: Via Ricasoli, 58/60, 50129 Firenze FI, Italy

Website: www.galleriaaccademiafirenze.beniculturali.it

BOBOLI GARDENS

The Boboli Gardens, situated behind the grand Pitti Palace, are a magnificent example of Italian Renaissance gardens and a veritable open-air museum. Spread over a vast area, these gardens are a masterful display of natural and architectural elements blending seamlessly. As you stroll through the myriad paths, you are greeted by an array of ornate fountains, sculptures, and grottos that date from the 16th to the 18th centuries. The gardens are not just a feast for the eyes; they offer a serene respite from the bustling city life, with lush greenery and tranquil water features. The design of the Boboli Gardens has inspired many royal gardens across Europe, including Versailles. The elevated position of the gardens provides breathtaking panoramic views of Florence and the rolling Tuscan hills, making it a perfect spot for photographers and nature lovers alike. The gardens also host various open-air concerts and events throughout the year, adding to their allure.

Tip: Plan to spend several hours exploring the extensive grounds. The Boboli Gardens are vast, and there is much to see, from the Amphitheatre with its Egyptian obelisk to the picturesque Viottolone pathway lined with cypresses. Consider visiting during different seasons to witness the changing beauty of the gardens.

Location: Piazza de' Pitti, 1, 50125 Firenze FI, Italy
Website: www.uffizi.it/en/boboli-garden

PITTI PALACE

The Pitti Palace, a majestic structure on the south bank of the Arno River, is a remarkable embodiment of Renaissance grandeur. Originally built for the Pitti family, it became the primary residence of the powerful Medici dynasty, signifying the shift of power from the old center to the Oltrarno. This imposing palace now hosts a series of museums, each offering a unique glimpse into the art and lifestyle of the period. The Palatine Gallery, with its sumptuous rooms adorned with paintings by Raphael, Titian, and Rubens, provides an insight into the opulence of the Medici court. The Royal Apartments display the luxury in which the Tuscan rulers lived, with their original furnishings and décor. Visitors can also explore the Costume Gallery, the Silver Museum, and the Porcelain Museum, each showcasing different aspects of artistic expression and craftsmanship. The architecture of the palace itself, with its simple yet majestic façade, is a statement of the power and wealth of Florence during the Renaissance.

Tip: To fully appreciate the extensive collections and the scale of the palace, it is advisable to dedicate at least half a day to your visit. The combined ticket, including access to the Boboli Gardens, not only offers a comprehensive experience but also allows you to enjoy the beauty of one of the most important green areas in Florence.

Location: Piazza de' Pitti, 1, 50125 Firenze FI, Italy
Website: www.uffizi.it/en/pitti-palace

BASILICA OF SANTA CROCE

The Basilica of Santa Croce, often referred to as the Temple of Italian Glories, stands as a monumental tribute to some of Italy's most influential figures. This Franciscan church, with its stunning Gothic façade, is the final resting place of legendary personalities such as Michelangelo, Galileo, Rossini, and Machiavelli, making it a pantheon of Italian history and culture. The interior of the basilica is equally impressive, adorned with a series of breathtaking frescoes by Giotto, depicting scenes from the life of St. Francis, and other significant artworks. Visitors are also drawn to the Pazzi Chapel, an architectural gem designed by Brunelleschi, which epitomizes the harmonious principles of Renaissance architecture. The church's cloisters offer a peaceful retreat, with their serene arcades and chapels. The Basilica of Santa Croce is not just a religious site; it is a repository of art, history, and architectural beauty, reflecting the rich cultural tapestry of Florence.

Tip: Allocate enough time to explore not only the church but also the attached Museum of the Opera di Santa Croce, which houses additional artworks and historical artifacts. The basilica occasionally hosts classical music concerts and cultural events, offering visitors an opportunity to experience the church's magnificent acoustics and atmosphere. Check the basilica's schedule ahead of your visit to catch these special events.

Location: Piazza di Santa Croce, 16, 50122 Firenze FI, Italy

Website: www.santacroceopera.it/en/

PIAZZA DELLA SIGNORIA

Piazza della Signoria, the historic and political hub of Florence, has been the focal point of the city's social and political life since the Middle Ages. This majestic L-shaped square is surrounded by some of the most significant buildings and statues in the city, making it an open-air museum in its own right. Dominated by the imposing Palazzo Vecchio, the square houses an array of statues including a replica of Michelangelo's David and the stunning Neptune Fountain. The adjacent Loggia dei Lanzi is an architectural masterpiece, showcasing a collection of Renaissance sculptures in an outdoor gallery setting. The square's vibrant and dynamic atmosphere is palpable, with locals and tourists mingling amongst street performers and historical reenactments. Piazza della Signoria is not just a square; it's a living testament to the rich history and artistry that define Florence, offering a glimpse into the city's soul.

Tip: For a more peaceful visit, aim to explore the square early in the morning or later in the evening when the crowds have dispersed. These times also offer a different perspective of the square's beauty, under the soft light of dawn or the dramatic illumination of night.

Don't miss the opportunity to visit the nearby Uffizi Gallery, which opens onto the square, to continue your journey through Florence's artistic heritage.

Location: P.za della Signoria, 50122 Firenze FI, Italy
Website: www.feelflorence.it/en/node/11533

MEDICI CHAPELS

The Medici Chapels in Florence are a magnificent mausoleum and a symbol of the Medici family's immense power and influence during the Renaissance. These chapels, forming part of the larger Basilica of San Lorenzo complex, are an architectural and artistic marvel. The New Sacristy, designed by Michelangelo, is particularly notable for its harmonious proportions and the sculptor's masterful works, including the tombs of Lorenzo and Giuliano de' Medici. Each sculpture in the chapel encapsulates Michelangelo's ability to capture human emotion and expression, making it a profound artistic experience. Additionally, the Chapel of the Princes, with its grand dome and lavish interior, adorned with precious stones and marbles, epitomizes the wealth and prestige of the Medici dynasty. This place is not just a burial site but a testament to the family's patronage of the arts and their central role in shaping the cultural landscape of Florence.

Tip: To fully appreciate the artistic significance of the chapels, consider using an audio guide or joining a guided tour. Also, as the chapels are a popular attraction, visiting early in the morning can help avoid the larger crowds that gather later in the day. The serene atmosphere of the chapels in the morning provides a more contemplative experience.

Location: P.za di Madonna degli Aldobrandini, 6, 50123 Firenze FI, Italy

Website: www.feelflorence.it/en/node/12241

BASILICA DI SAN LORENZO

The Basilica di San Lorenzo, steeped in history and art, is not only one of Florence's oldest churches but also a significant landmark in the heart of the city. It served as the parish church for the influential Medici family, reflecting their deep connection to the religious and cultural life of Florence. Designed by the renowned architect Filippo Brunelleschi, the church's interior is a testament to the elegance and balance of Renaissance architecture, marked by clean lines and a sense of harmonious proportion. Beyond its religious significance, the Basilica di San Lorenzo is home to the Laurentian Library, an architectural masterpiece by Michelangelo. This library is a treasure trove of historic manuscripts and early books, showcasing Michelangelo's innovative design in its reading room and staircase. The contrast between the church's relatively modest exterior and the artistic richness within makes it a fascinating destination for those interested in the interplay between art, architecture, and history.

Tip: The unassuming exterior belies the artistic and architectural wonders inside, so ensure to explore the interior fully. The Laurentian Library, with its limited opening hours, requires planning; check the timings before your visit. Additionally, the Medici Chapels, located within the basilica complex, are also worth visiting to complete your experience of this historical site.

Location: Piazza di San Lorenzo, 9, 50123 Firenze FI, Italy
Website: www.sanlorenzofirenze.it/en/

MUSEO DELL'OPERA DEL DUOMO

The Museo dell'Opera del Duomo, nestled in the shadow of the magnificent Florence Cathedral, serves as a custodian to the artistic masterpieces originally created for the city's most iconic religious structures: the Cathedral, Baptistery, and Giotto's Bell Tower. This museum is a treasure trove of Renaissance art, showcasing original sculptures by luminaries such as Michelangelo and Donatello. Among its most prized possessions are the original panels of the Gates of Paradise from the Baptistery, crafted by Lorenzo Ghiberti, which stand as a testament to the artistic genius of the Renaissance. The museum not only offers a comprehensive view of the art associated with the Duomo complex but also provides context and insights into the historical and religious significance of these works. Visitors can explore a variety of sculptures, reliefs, and other artifacts, each telling a part of the rich story of Florence's religious and artistic heritage. The museum's design, with its spacious layout and natural lighting, enhances the viewing experience, allowing these historic works to be seen in a new light.

Tip: To truly appreciate the museum's extensive collection, plan to spend several hours here. Don't miss the opportunity to visit the rooftop terrace, which provides a unique and breathtaking view of the Florence Cathedral and the surrounding cityscape – a perfect spot for capturing memorable photos of your visit.

Location: Piazza del Duomo, 9, 50122 Firenze FI, Italy
Website: www.duomo.firenze.it/en

HIDDEN GEMS AND LESSER-KNOWN SIGHTS IN FLORENCE
BRANCACCI CHAPEL

The Brancacci Chapel, located within the Church of Santa Maria del Carmine in Florence, is a hidden gem that holds a significant place in the history of Renaissance art. Renowned for its remarkable frescoes by Masaccio and Masolino, the chapel is often referred to as the "Sistine Chapel of the early Renaissance" for its artistic importance. These frescoes, depicting various scenes from the life of St. Peter, are celebrated for their groundbreaking use of perspective and realistic portrayal of emotion and human figures. Masaccio's contributions, in particular, mark a dramatic shift from the Gothic to the Renaissance artistic style, making the chapel a crucial site for anyone interested in the evolution of Western art. The frescoes' vivid storytelling and the chapel's serene atmosphere provide a moving and intimate artistic experience, offering a glimpse into the genius that would shape Renaissance art.

Tip: The chapel's small size and the delicate nature of the frescoes limit the number of visitors allowed at a time. To ensure your visit, it's recommended to book tickets in advance, especially during high tourist season. A visit to the Brancacci Chapel is often a highlight for art lovers and can be a profound experience for all visitors.

Location: Piazza del Carmine, 14, 50124 Firenze FI, Italy
Website:www.museumsinflorence.com/musei/Brancacci_chapel.html

BASILICA OF SANTO SPIRITO

The Basilica of Santo Spirito, situated in the lesser-traveled but equally charming Oltrarno district of Florence, is a masterpiece of Renaissance architecture by the legendary Filippo Brunelleschi. Despite its relatively plain façade, the church's interior is a revelation of serene beauty and harmonious proportions, characteristic of Brunelleschi's architectural style. Inside, art enthusiasts can admire an array of artworks, including pieces by Filippino Lippi and other Renaissance masters. The church's ambiance is one of tranquility and spiritual contemplation, offering a respite from the more crowded sites of Florence. The Piazza Santo Spirito, in front of the church, pulsates with local life, featuring a vibrant mix of artisanal shops, quaint cafes, and traditional trattorias. This lively square is a window into the everyday life of Florentines, providing a more authentic experience of the city.

Tip: For a truly local experience, plan your visit to coincide with the monthly antiques market held in the Piazza Santo Spirito. This event is a treasure trove for unique finds and offers a chance to experience the lively community atmosphere. The evenings in the piazza are also particularly enjoyable, with locals gathering for apéritifs and socializing, making it a perfect spot for visitors to immerse themselves in the local culture.

Location: Piazza Santo Spirito, 30, 50125 Firenze FI, Italy
Website: www.basilicasantospirito.it/en

SAN MINIATO AL MONTE

The Basilica of San Miniato al Monte, crowning one of the highest points in Florence, is not only a religious sanctuary but also a place of unparalleled beauty and peace. Over a thousand years old, this Romanesque church is acclaimed for its striking geometrically patterned marble façade, which exemplifies the elegance of Italian medieval architecture. The interior is equally captivating, adorned with intricate mosaics that shimmer in the natural light, creating a serene and contemplative atmosphere. Beyond its architectural and artistic wonders, San Miniato al Monte offers some of the most spectacular panoramic views of Florence, stretching out over the red-tiled roofs to the rolling Tuscan hills beyond. The church's historic cemetery adds to the site's aura of timeless tranquility. Visiting San Miniato al Monte provides a unique opportunity to step back from the energy of the city and immerse oneself in a place that has been a spiritual haven for centuries.

Tip: To enhance your experience, plan to visit during the evening vespers when the monks of San Miniato chant Gregorian hymns. The combination of the chants and the church's acoustics offers a truly transcendent experience. Additionally, the walk up to the basilica, though steep, is rewarded with breathtaking views and a less crowded path to explore Florence's rich history and beauty.

Location: Via delle Porte Sante, 34, 50125 Firenze FI, Italy

Website: www.sanminiatoalmonte.it

PALAZZO MEDICI RICCARDI

The Palazzo Medici Riccardi stands as a testament to the wealth and influence of the Medici family, who were instrumental in shaping the Renaissance in Florence. Constructed in the 15th century, this Renaissance palace boasts a striking stone façade that exudes elegance and grandeur. The highlight of the palace is the Magi Chapel, where the walls are adorned with exquisite frescoes by Benozzo Gozzoli. These vibrant frescoes depict the procession of the Magi and are celebrated for their vivid colors and detailed portrayal of the characters, offering a glimpse into the artistic and cultural splendor of the Renaissance period. The palace's interior, with its opulent decor and intricate artworks, transports visitors back to the height of Medici power. Additionally, the palace's courtyard is a serene oasis, featuring a classical design that provides a quiet respite from the bustling city. A visit to the Palazzo Medici Riccardi is not just about exploring a historic building; it's an immersive experience into the legacy of one of the most influential families in Italian history.

Tip: Take time to explore the lesser-known areas of the palace, including the beautifully designed courtyard, which offers a tranquil spot to reflect on the history and art you've experienced. The palace occasionally hosts art exhibitions and cultural events, so check their schedule for any ongoing or upcoming events during your visit.

Location: Via Camillo Cavour, 3, 50129 Firenze FI, Italy
Website: www.palazzomediciriccardi.it/en/

MUSEO HORNE

Tucked away in the heart of Florence, the Museo Horne is a delightful escape into the world of Renaissance domestic life. Established by the English art historian Herbert Horne, this museum offers an intimate look at the artistic and everyday life of the Florentine elite during the Renaissance era. Set within a beautifully preserved 15th-century palazzo, the museum houses a remarkable collection of Renaissance art, sculptures, and furniture. Each room in the museum is meticulously arranged to mirror a typical home of the period, providing visitors with a tangible sense of the past. The collection includes notable works of art, ceramics, and an impressive array of period furniture, each piece telling its own story of craftsmanship and beauty. The Museo Horne stands out for its unique focus on the domestic aspects of Renaissance life, offering a different perspective from the grand public art typically associated with the period.

Tip: The quiet and less crowded atmosphere of the Museo Horne makes it an ideal spot for those who wish to delve deeply into the art and history without the rush and bustle of more tourist-heavy locations. It's a perfect destination for art lovers and history enthusiasts who are looking for a more tranquil and reflective museum experience in Florence.

Location: Via dei Benci, 6, 50122 Firenze FI, Italy
Website: www.museohorne.it/en/

PALAZZO DELL'ANTELLA

Overlooking the famous Piazza Santa Croce, Palazzo dell'Antella stands as a captivating testament to Florentine baroque architecture and art. Its striking feature is the elaborately frescoed façade, a rarity in Florence, which captures the eye with its vivid colors and intricate designs. Painted by various artists in the early 17th century, these frescoes depict a fascinating array of historical and mythological scenes, each a masterpiece in its own right. The building's exterior serves as a canvas, telling stories that blend reality with fantasy, and history with legend. Palazzo dell'Antella is a hidden gem that many visitors to Florence often overlook, yet it offers a unique and enchanting glimpse into the artistic creativity of the baroque period. The square itself is bustling with activity, but the Palazzo offers a moment of artistic wonder amidst the lively atmosphere of Piazza Santa Croce.

Tip: Take your time to observe and appreciate the detailed artwork on the façade. Each panel tells a different story and reflects the rich artistic heritage of Florence. Early morning or late afternoon light can provide the best illumination for viewing and photographing the frescoes. For art enthusiasts, this building is a must-see for its unique contribution to the city's architectural landscape

Location: Piazza di Santa Croce, 21, 50122 Firenze FI, Italy
Website: www.feelflorence.it/en/node/47734

MUSEO GALILEO

Nestled in the heart of Florence, the Museo Galileo is a temple to scientific exploration and discovery, offering a unique perspective on the city's rich history. This museum, dedicated to the history of science, houses an impressive array of scientific instruments from the Renaissance to the modern era, with a special focus on the groundbreaking tools used by Galileo Galilei. As visitors walk through its halls, they encounter telescopes, astrolabes, and other devices that trace the evolution of scientific thought and practice. The Museo Galileo not only celebrates the genius of its namesake but also the contributions of numerous Italian scientists who have played pivotal roles in various fields of study. This museum is more than a collection of artifacts; it's a journey through the history of human curiosity and ingenuity. With interactive exhibits and digital reconstructions, the Museo Galileo brings to life the thrilling quest for knowledge that has driven humanity for centuries.

Tip: The museum's interactive exhibits are particularly engaging for younger visitors, making it an excellent choice for families. Be sure to explore the digital reconstructions, which provide a captivating and immersive way to understand the significance of these historical scientific instruments. The museum also offers temporary exhibitions and educational workshops that are worth checking out.

Location: Piazza dei Giudici, 1, 50122 Firenze FI, Italy
Website: www.museogalileo.it/en/

STROZZI PALACE FOUNDATION

Situated in the heart of Florence, the Strozzi Palace Foundation is an exquisite blend of historical grandeur and contemporary artistry. Housed within the magnificent Palazzo Strozzi, a stunning example of Renaissance architecture, the foundation is celebrated for its dynamic and high-caliber contemporary art exhibitions. The palazzo itself, with its spacious courtyards and elegant rooms, provides a striking backdrop for modern art installations and exhibitions, creating a fascinating dialogue between the old and the new. Visitors to the Strozzi Palace Foundation are treated to a unique cultural experience that juxtaposes the timeless beauty of Renaissance design with cutting-edge artistic expression. The foundation's commitment to showcasing contemporary artists and thematic exhibitions makes it a pivotal space for art lovers and those intrigued by the evolving nature of artistic expression. Whether it's multimedia installations, modern sculptures, or avant-garde paintings, the Strozzi Palace Foundation offers a refreshing perspective on contemporary art in a city renowned for its historical art treasures.

Tip: To make the most of your visit, keep an eye on the foundation's website for information about current and upcoming exhibitions. Some exhibitions might be time-sensitive or feature internationally renowned artists, making advance booking a good idea. The courtyard of Palazzo Strozzi is a beautiful and tranquil space, perfect for a moment of reflection or a leisurely break amidst your exploration of Florence.
Location: Piazza degli Strozzi, 50123 Firenze FI, Italy
Website: www.palazzostrozzi.org/en/

MUSEUM OF ZOOLOGY AND NATURAL HISTORY

The Specola Museum, part of the Museum of Natural History of the University of Florence, is a hidden gem that offers an intriguing glimpse into the world of zoology and natural history. Located in a historic Palazzo, this museum houses an extensive collection of taxidermy, anatomical waxes, and botanical specimens, making it one of the most important natural history museums in Europe. The Specola is especially famous for its collection of anatomical waxes, which are both fascinating and artistically significant, providing insights into medical knowledge and practices of the past. The museum's zoological section showcases a wide variety of animal specimens, offering a comprehensive view of biodiversity. The Specola Museum provides a unique and educational experience, allowing visitors to explore the natural world and its wonders in a historical context.

Tip: While the museum's anatomical waxes are a major draw, don't overlook the other collections, including the fascinating array of taxidermy. The museum is less crowded than other tourist attractions in Florence, offering a more peaceful and contemplative experience. Photography enthusiasts will find many intriguing

Location: Via Romana, 17, 50125 Firenze FI, Italy
Website: www.sma.unifi.it/index.html?newlang=eng

PARKS AND GARDENS IN FLORENCE

CASCINE PARK

Cascine Park, Florence's largest public green space, is a haven of tranquility and recreation for both locals and tourists alike. Extending along the scenic banks of the Arno River, this sprawling park offers an idyllic setting for a variety of outdoor activities. Visitors can enjoy its expansive meadows, perfect for picnics and sunbathing, or stroll along the shaded tree-lined avenues. The park also features several sports facilities, making it a popular spot for jogging, cycling, and tennis. Every Tuesday, Cascine Park transforms into a bustling marketplace, where vendors sell everything from fresh local produce to clothing and accessories. Throughout the year, the park serves as a venue for a range of events, including concerts, festivals, and cultural gatherings, making it a vibrant part of Florence's community life. Whether you're looking to relax in nature, engage in sports, or immerse yourself in local culture, Cascine Park offers a diverse range of experiences set against the backdrop of Florence's stunning natural beauty.

Tip: For a truly local experience, visit the park on a Tuesday morning to explore the lively market. It's an excellent opportunity to sample local Tuscan flavors and find unique souvenirs. Additionally, the park's size and varied landscapes make it perfect for long, leisurely walks or bike rides, especially in the early morning or late afternoon when the light is most beautiful.

Location: Piazzale delle Cascine, 50144 Firenze FI, Italy
Website: www.feelflorence.it/en/node/12107

IRIS GARDEN (GIARDINO DELL'IRIS)

The Iris Garden, located near Piazzale Michelangelo, is a splendid garden dedicated to the cultivation of irises, the symbol of Florence. With over 1,500 varieties, the garden becomes a kaleidoscope of colors in bloom, particularly in May when the Iris Competition takes place. This lesser-known garden offers not only a visual delight with its colorful displays but also a serene atmosphere with stunning views of the city.

Tip: The garden is only open for a few weeks during the blooming season in May, making this a unique and timely experience for visitors to Florence during this period.

Location: Giardino dell'Iris50125 Firenze FI, Italy
Website: www.feelflorence.it/en/node/12092

PARCO SAN DONATO

Parco San Donato is a modern and expansive green space located in the northern part of Florence. This park, a relatively new addition to the city's landscape, is characterized by its wide open fields, contemporary art installations, and children's play areas. It's an ideal spot for families, joggers, and those seeking a quiet escape from the urban environment. The park's design integrates open lawns, walking paths, and sitting areas, offering a refreshing and relaxing outdoor experience. Parco San Donato is a testament to Florence's commitment to green urban spaces, combining functionality with aesthetic appeal.

Tip: The park is perfect for a picnic or a leisurely walk. Its spacious layout makes it less crowded than other parks in Florence, providing a peaceful atmosphere.

Location: Via Sandro Pertini, 2/9, 50127 Firenze FI, Italy
Website: www.feelflorence.it/en/node/16893

GIARDINO DELLA GHERARDESCA

The Giardino Della Gherardesca is a hidden jewel in Florence, offering a serene and lush retreat from the city's bustling atmosphere. Located within the grounds of the Four Seasons Hotel, this historic garden is one of the largest private parks in Florence. Its origins date back to the 15th century, and it showcases an exquisite mix of Renaissance and English landscape styles. Visitors can wander through a maze of pathways, discovering ancient trees, ornate fountains, and statues that enhance the garden's enchanting ambience. The garden also features a small temple, a neoclassical conservatory, and beautifully manicured lawns, making it a perfect setting for a peaceful stroll or a moment of contemplation amidst nature's splendor. The Giardino Della Gherardesca is a testament to Florence's rich horticultural history and provides a unique opportunity to experience the city's aristocratic past.

Tip: While the garden is privately owned, it is accessible to the public through the hotel. Visiting during spring and early summer is particularly rewarding when the flowers are in full bloom.

Location: Borgo Pinti, 99, 50121 Firenze FI, Italy
Website: www.fourseasons.com/florence/

ROSE GARDEN

The Rose Garden, situated below Piazzale Michelangelo, is a delightful spot that offers a tranquil environment and a splendid variety of roses. With over 400 varieties of roses, along with numerous other plants and artistic sculptures, the garden is a feast for the senses. It's particularly stunning in May and June when the roses are in full bloom.

Tip: Visit during sunset for a spectacular view of Florence bathed in golden light, with the fragrance of roses adding to the ambiance.
Location: Viale Giuseppe Poggi, 2, 50125 Firenze FI, Italy
Website: www.visittuscany.com/en/attractions/the-rose-garden-inflorence/

BARDINI GARDEN

The Bardini Garden, often less visited than the Boboli Gardens, is a hidden gem offering lush greenery, colorful flowers, and spectacular views over Florence. This historic garden, restored to its former glory, features a baroque staircase, fountains, and a wisteria pergola. It's a serene and picturesque place, perfect for a leisurely walk or a quiet moment of reflection.

Tip: The garden's wisteria blooms beautifully in spring, making it an ideal time for a visit. Combine your visit with the adjacent Villa Bardini for a fuller experience.
Location: Via de' Bardi, 1, 50125 Firenze FI, Italy
Website: www.villabardini.it/en/

FLORENCE'S CULINARY SCENE

OSTERIA DEL CINGHIALE BIANCO

Osteria del Cinghiale Bianco, located in the heart of the Oltrarno district, is a quintessential Florentine eatery known for its traditional Tuscan cuisine. The restaurant, with its rustic charm and warm atmosphere, specializes in dishes featuring wild boar, as its name suggests. Their menu also includes a variety of classic Tuscan recipes, all prepared with fresh, locally-sourced ingredients.

Tip: Try their signature wild boar ragù, a flavorful and authentic Tuscan dish. Reservations are recommended, especially for dinner.

Location: Borgo S. Jacopo, 43, 50125 Firenze FI, Italy
Website: www.cinghialebianco.com

TRATTORIA MARIO

Trattoria Mario is a historic eatery near the San Lorenzo market, famous for offering an authentic Florentine dining experience. This family-run trattoria, established in 1953, serves simple yet delicious Tuscan fare in a bustling, communal setting. Known for their Florentine steak and traditional pasta dishes, Trattoria Mario provides a taste of local life and cuisine at its most genuine.

Tip: The trattoria is only open for lunch and can get quite crowded, so be prepared to share a table with other diners. Arriving early is advisable.

Location: Via Rosina, 2r, 50123 Firenze FI, Italy
Website: www.trattoriamario.com/

ENOTECA PINCHIORRI

For a luxury dining experience, Enoteca Pinchiorri is unparalleled in Florence. This Michelin-starred restaurant is renowned for its exquisite cuisine, extensive wine selection, and impeccable service. The menu showcases innovative interpretations of Tuscan and Italian dishes, created with the finest ingredients. The elegant setting and refined atmosphere make it ideal for a special occasion.

Tip: The tasting menu is a great way to experience the chef's culinary artistry. Remember, the dress code is formal, and reservations are essential.

Location: Via Ghibellina, 87, 50122 Firenze FI, Italy

Website: www.enotecapinchiorri.it/?lang=en

ALL'ANTICO VINAIO

All'Antico Vinaio is a beloved street food spot in Florence, famous for its scrumptious sandwiches. This small, unassuming shop offers a variety of sandwiches made with freshly baked bread and filled with high-quality local ingredients like cured meats, cheeses, and spreads. It's a budget-friendly option that doesn't compromise on flavor and quality, perfect for a quick and satisfying meal.

Tip: The lines can be long, but they move quickly. Try their famous 'schiacciata' sandwiches, especially the ones with truffle cream.

Location: Via dei Neri, 65r, 50122 Firenze FI, Italy

Website: www.allanticovinaio.com

BISTECCA ALLA FIORENTINA

Bistecca alla Fiorentina, or Florentine Steak, is more than just a dish; it's a culinary symbol of Florence. This thick cut of T-bone steak, usually from the Chianina or Maremmana breeds of cattle, is grilled over a wood or charcoal fire, seasoned simply with salt, pepper, and a touch of olive oil, and served rare. The steak's rich flavor and tender texture make it a favorite among meat lovers.

Where to Try: Trattoria Mario and Osteria del Cinghiale Bianco are excellent choices for authentic Bistecca alla Fiorentina.
Tip: This dish is typically ordered by weight and shared among multiple people, making it a social dining experience. It's best enjoyed with a side of Tuscan beans or a fresh salad.

CANTUCCINI CON VIN SANTO

Cantuccini con Vin Santo is a traditional Tuscan dessert consisting of cantuccini, almond biscuits that are twice-baked and crunchy, paired with Vin Santo, a sweet dessert wine. The ritual of dipping cantuccini into Vin Santo, enjoying the softened biscuit infused with the wine's flavors, is a quintessential Florentine experience.
Where to Try: Most local cafes and dessert shops in Florence serve this classic dessert. Cafes around Piazza della Signoria or Piazza del Duomo are great for enjoying this treat.
Tip: Dip the cantuccini briefly in Vin Santo to soften them slightly and enhance their flavor without making them too soggy.

CHIANTI WINE

Chianti, a red wine from Tuscany, is famous worldwide and an integral part of the culinary scene in Florence. Characterized by its bright ruby color, Chianti is primarily made from Sangiovese grapes and offers a range of flavors from robust and rustic to round and fruit-forward. Tasting Chianti in Florence, where it pairs perfectly with the local cuisine, is a delightful experience for wine enthusiasts.

Where to Try: Enoteca Pinchiorri boasts an extensive selection of Chianti wines. For a more casual setting, try a local enoteca or wine bar in the city center.

Tip: Consider visiting a wine bar or enoteca that offers wine tasting sessions or pairings with local cheeses and meats for a comprehensive Chianti experience.

RIBOLLITA

Ribollita is a hearty Tuscan soup that epitomizes the concept of Italian peasant cooking. Made from cannellini beans, vegetables, and stale bread, this thick soup is a staple of Tuscan cuisine. Originally a way to use up leftovers, Ribollita is now celebrated for its flavors, nourishing qualities, and simplicity. It's particularly popular in the colder months and is known for its comforting and rustic appeal.

Where to Try: Trattorias and osterias throughout Florence serve authentic Ribollita, with each chef adding their personal touch to this traditional recipe.

Tip: Ribollita is best enjoyed in a relaxed setting, paired with a glass of local red wine and savored as a warming, hearty meal.

PAPPA AL POMODORO

Pappa al Pomodoro is a traditional Florentine dish made from tomatoes, bread, olive oil, garlic, and basil. This thick, bread-based soup is a testament to the Tuscan tradition of using simple, high-quality ingredients. The dish is both humble and delicious, with the ripe tomatoes and fresh basil highlighting the flavors of Tuscany.

Where to Try: Available in many local eateries across Florence, especially those specializing in traditional Tuscan cuisine.

Tip: Pappa al Pomodoro is typically served hot, but it can also be enjoyed at room temperature, making it a versatile dish for any season.

LAMPREDOTTO SANDWICH

The Lampredotto sandwich is a classic street food item in Florence, made from the fourth stomach of a cow, slow-cooked until tender, and served in a crusty roll. This sandwich is typically topped with a spicy sauce or a green sauce made with herbs, providing a unique and robust flavor. Eating a Lampredotto sandwich is a quintessential Florentine experience and a must-try for adventurous foodies.

Where to Try: Street food vendors and markets around Florence, especially in the San Lorenzo market, are the best places to find authentic Lampredotto sandwiches.

Tip: Enjoy your Lampredotto sandwich standing up at a street vendor like the locals, paired with a glass of local red wine or a cold beer for the full experience.

SHOPPING IN FLORENCE

MERCATO CENTRALE

The Mercato Centrale, located in the San Lorenzo neighborhood, is a culinary haven for food lovers. The first floor of this historic market is a traditional food market selling fresh produce, meats, cheeses, and other Tuscan specialties. The upper floor has been transformed into a modern food hall where visitors can enjoy a variety of local and international cuisines.

Tip: Visit the market for lunch to experience a wide range of food offerings. It's also a great place to buy high-quality local products offerings. It's also a great place to buy high-quality local products like olive oil and balsamic vinegar.

Location: Via dell'Ariento, 50123 Firenze FI, Italy
Website: www.mercatocentrale.com/florence/

VIA DE' TORNABUONI

Via de' Tornabuoni is Florence's most famous shopping street, known for its high-end boutiques and designer stores. This elegant street houses renowned luxury brands, offering the latest in fashion, jewelry, and accessories. It's not just a shopping destination but also a place to admire the stunning architecture of the surrounding buildings and the chic atmosphere of the city.

Tip: Even if luxury shopping isn't your intention, a stroll along Via de' Tornabuoni is worthwhile for window shopping and enjoying the sophisticated ambiance.

Location: Via de' Tornabuoni, 50123 Firenze FI, Italy
Website: www.visittuscany.com/en/attractions/via-de-tornabuoni/

OFFICINA PROFUMO-FARMACEUTICA DI SANTA MARIA NOVELLA

Officina Profumo-Farmaceutica di Santa Maria Novella is one of the world's oldest pharmacies, dating back to the 13th century. This historic store offers a range of unique products, including perfumes, soaps, and skincare items made with traditional methods and natural ingredients. The enchanting interior, with its antique furniture and frescoes, makes shopping here a truly unique experience.

Tip: Take time to explore the history of the pharmacy through its products. The Rose Water and Potpourri are classic picks for a unique souvenir.
Location: Via della Scala, 16, 50123 Firenze FI, Italy
Website: www.eu.smnovella.com

VIA DEI CALZAIUOLI

Via dei Calzaiuoli is one of the main shopping streets in Florence, offering a mix of high-end and local shops. This bustling pedestrian street runs between the Duomo and Piazza della Signoria and is lined with stores selling clothing, accessories, and souvenirs. It's a great place to shop for both luxury brands and affordable items, all while enjoying the historic ambiance of central Florence.

Tip: Be sure to venture into the side streets and alleys off Via dei Calzaiuoli, where you can find smaller, independent shops and artisanal boutiques.
Location: Via dei Calzaiuoli 50122 Firenze FI, Italy
Website: www.visittuscany.com/en/attractions/via-dei-calzaiuoli/

SANT'AMBROGIO MARKET

Sant'Ambrogio Market offers a genuine slice of Florentine life. This less touristy market is bustling with locals shopping for fresh produce, cheeses, and Tuscan delicacies. Both an indoor food market and an outdoor area with various goods create a lively atmosphere. It's the perfect place to experience the everyday culture of Florence, offering a chance to mingle with locals and taste authentic flavors.

Tip: Visit in the morning for the freshest selections and consider stopping at nearby cafes for a traditional Italian coffee experience after exploring the market.

Location: Piazza Lorenzo Ghiberti, 50122 Firenze FI, Italy
Website: www.mercatosantambrogio.it/?lang=en

IL PAPIRO

Il Papiro celebrates Florence's traditional art of paper making. This charming shop features handcrafted paper products, including elegant stationery, journals, and unique marbled paper. The store is a treasure trove of artisanal craftsmanship, perfect for finding special souvenirs or gifts that embody Florentine artistry.

Visitors can often witness the fascinating paper-marbling process.

Tip: Inquire about paper-making demonstrations to gain deeper insight into this ancient craft, making your visit both educational and memorable.

Location: Via Camillo Cavour, 49, 50129 Firenze FI, Italy, and other various locations across the city
Website: www.ilpapirofirenze.it

FAMILY-FRIENDLY ACTIVITIES IN FLORENCE

PALAZZO VECCHIO MUSEUM

The Palazzo Vecchio Museum offers interactive tours and activities designed specifically for families with children. Located in the historic Palazzo Vecchio, this museum provides a fun and educational experience where kids can learn about art and history in an engaging way. Activities include treasure hunts, costume workshops, and storytelling sessions, all set within the fascinating rooms of the palace.

Tip: Check the museum's schedule for special family-friendly events and activities, which are often available, especially during school holidays.
Location: Piazza della Signoria, 50122 Firenze FI, Italy
Website: www.musefirenze.it/en/musei/museo-di-palazzo-vecchio/

GALILEO MUSEUM

The Galileo Museum is a fascinating place for families, especially those interested in science and astronomy. The museum showcases an extensive collection of scientific instruments, including Galileo's telescopes and tools, offering insight into the history of science. Interactive exhibits and multimedia displays make the experience more engaging for children, helping them understand the significance of Galileo's work.

Tip: The museum offers educational workshops and guided tours suitable for children, which can be a great way to enhance their learning experience.
Location: Piazza dei Giudici, 1, 50122 Firenze FI, Italy
Website: www.museogalileo.it/en/

ADVENTURE PARK IL GIGANTE

Just outside Florence, Adventure Park Il Gigante offers an exhilarating outdoor experience for the whole family. With various aerial trails set in a beautiful forest, it caters to different age groups and skill levels. Activities include zip-lines, rope bridges, and climbing challenges, all under the supervision of trained staff.

Tip: Wear comfortable clothing and shoes suitable for physical activities.

The park is a great way to combine fun and physical exercise in a natural setting.
Location: Via Fiorentina, 50036 Pratolino FI, Italy
Website: www.parcoavventurailgigante.it/en/

CAROUSEL AT PIAZZA DELLA REPUBBLICA

The antique carousel in Piazza della Repubblica is a charming attraction for younger children. This traditional merry-go-round, with beautifully decorated horses and carriages, provides a whimsical ride in the heart of Florence. It's a simple yet delightful experience, bringing joy to children and nostalgia to adults.

Tip: The carousel is a perfect stop after exploring the nearby historical sites and shopping streets. The piazza also has several cafes where families can relax and enjoy the lively atmosphere.
Location: Piazza della Repubblica, 50123 Firenze FI, Italy.
Website: www.feelflorence.it/en/node/16768

GIARDINO DELL'ORTICOLTURA

The Giardino dell'Orticoltura is a lesser-known gem in Florence, offering a peaceful green space with a variety of plants and flowers. The garden features a large playground, making it ideal for families with children. It's a perfect spot for a relaxing day out, allowing kids to play and explore in a safe and beautiful environment.

Tip: The garden often hosts flower shows and other family-friendly events, especially in the spring and summer months, adding an extra layer of interest to your visit.
Location: Via Vittorio Emanuele II, 4, 50139 Firenze FI, Italy
Website: www.giardinoartecultura.it/

CHILDREN'S ART WORKSHOP AT THE UFFIZI

The Uffizi Gallery offers special art workshops for children, providing a unique opportunity for young visitors to engage with art. Under the guidance of experienced educators, children can participate in various activities, from painting to sculpture, inspired by the masterpieces in the Uffizi. It's an excellent way for kids to explore their creativity while learning about art history.

Tip: Book the workshops in advance, as they are popular and spaces are limited. These activities are a great way to make art more accessible and enjoyable for children.
Location: Piazzale degli Uffizi, 6, 50122 Firenze FI, Italy
Website: www.uffizi.it/en/ts/families

FLORENCE BY NIGHT

ILLUMINATED MONUMENTS AND EVENING STROLLS

PIAZZALE MICHELANGELO

Piazzale Michelangelo offers one of the most stunning views of Florence, especially enchanting at night when the city lights up. The panoramic view includes major landmarks like the Duomo, Palazzo Vecchio, and the Arno River. It's a popular spot for both locals and tourists to enjoy the evening ambiance and take in the breathtaking scenery.

Tip: Sunset is particularly magical at Piazzale Michelangelo. Consider bringing a small picnic to enjoy the view as the city transitions from day to night.
Location: Piazzale Michelangelo, 50125 Firenze FI, Italy
Website: www.feelflorence.it/en/node/12697

FLORENCE CATHEDRAL

The Florence Cathedral, or the Duomo, is an awe-inspiring sight by day and even more so at night when it's illuminated. The cathedral's intricate façade and the grandeur of Brunelleschi's dome lit up against the night sky is a must-see. The lighting accentuates the architectural details, making it a perfect subject for night photography.

Tip: The piazza around the Duomo is less crowded in the evening, offering a more peaceful experience of this magnificent structure. **Location**: Piazza del Duomo, 50122 Firenze FI, Italy **Website**: https://duomo.firenze.it/en/home

PONTE VECCHIO

The iconic Ponte Vecchio, known for its medieval stone arches and jewelry shops, takes on a romantic and mystical charm at night. The reflections of its lights on the Arno River create a magical atmosphere. Walking across the bridge and along the riverbanks in the evening offers a picturesque experience of Florence's enduring beauty.

Tip: For a quieter experience, visit the bridge after dinner when the crowds have thinned.
Location: Ponte Vecchio, 50125 Firenze FI, Italy
Website: www.feelflorence.it/en/node/12057

AN EVENING STROLL ALONG THE ARNO RIVER

A leisurely evening stroll along the Arno River is a delightful way to experience Florence's serene side. The river, with its historic bridges and the reflections of the city lights, creates a romantic and tranquil ambiance. Walking along the riverbanks, you'll pass by several notable sights and get a different perspective of the city.

Tip: For a unique experience, consider a late evening walk starting from Ponte Vecchio and heading towards the less crowded areas along the river.

Location: Lungarno (riverbanks of the Arno), Florence, Italy
Website: www.feelflorence.it/en/node/38848

BARS AND PUBS

VOLUME BAR

Volume Bar, located in the lively Santo Spirito neighborhood, is a favorite among locals and tourists alike. Known for its eclectic decor and vibrant atmosphere, this bar offers a wide selection of drinks and often hosts live music performances. It's a great place to mingle with locals and enjoy the laid-back Florentine nightlife.

Tip: Try their artisanal cocktails or local wines. Arrive early if you want to grab a seat, as it can get crowded, especially on weekends.

Location: Piazza Santo Spirito, 3, 50125 Firenze FI, Italy

Website: www.volume.fi.it

LA CITÉ LIBRARY BAR

La Cité Library Bar is a unique and cozy spot, ideal for book lovers and those looking for a relaxed evening. This bar-library hybrid is filled with books and offers a warm and inviting atmosphere. They serve a variety of drinks, including coffee, wine, and cocktails, and often host cultural events and live music.

Tip: Explore their book collection and enjoy the combination of a good read with a delicious drink. Check their schedule for any special events happening during your visit.

Location: Borgo S. Frediano, 20/R, 50124 Firenze FI, Italy

Website: www.lacitelibreria.info

MAYDAY CLUB

he Mayday Club is a charming and quirky cocktail bar known for its vintage airplane-themed decor. It offers a wide range of creative cocktails and a welcoming ambiance, making it a perfect spot for an enjoyable night out. The friendly bartenders and the intimate setting add to the overall experience.

Tip: Don't hesitate to ask the bartenders for recommendations. They're known for their mixology skills and can whip up personalized drinks based on your preferences.
Location: Via Dante Alighieri, 16/r, 50122 Firenze FI, Italy
Website: www.maydayclub.it

THE RED GARTER

The Red Garter, established in 1962, is one of Florence's oldest American bars and a popular spot among international visitors and students. Known for its lively atmosphere, it offers a full bar, restaurant, and even a karaoke stage. It's a great place to have a fun night out, especially if you're looking to meet new people.

Tip: Check out their karaoke nights if you're in the mood for some singing. The Red Garter is also known for its American-style burgers, perfect for a late-night snack.

Location: Via dei Benci, 33, R, 50122 Firenze FI, Italy
Website: www.redgarter1962.com/en/

NIGHTCLUBS AND DANCE CLUBS

YAB NIGHTCLUB

YAB Nightclub is one of the most popular nightclubs in Florence, known for its stylish ambiance and energetic vibe. This club attracts a young and fashionable crowd and is famous for its themed nights and guest DJs. With a spacious dance floor and a variety of music genres, YAB is a go-to destination for dance enthusiasts.

Tip: Dress to impress, as the club has a strict dress code. Check their website or social media pages for information on special events or guest DJ nights.
Location: Via dei Sassetti, 5/r, 50123 Firenze FI, Italy
Website: www.yab.it

DABADABA

Space Club is one of Florence's largest and most dynamic nightclubs, offering a high-energy nightlife experience. The club features cutting-edge sound and lighting systems, and regularly hosts both local and international DJs. It's a great place for those looking to party late into the night in a lively and vibrant setting.

Tip: The club is known for its diverse music nights, so check the schedule in advance to find a night that suits your musical taste.

Location: Via Palazzuolo, 37, 50123 Firenze FI, Italy
Website: www.facebook.com/spacefirenze2/

OTEL VARIETÉ

Otel Varieté offers a unique clubbing experience in Florence, combining dinner shows with a nightclub atmosphere. Known for its extravagant performances and elegant setting, Otel provides a night full of entertainment. Post-dinner, the venue transforms into a lively club where you can dance the night away.

Tip: Consider booking a dinner show for a complete experience. It's an excellent choice for those looking for a night out with a mix of entertainment and dancing.
Location: Via Generale C. A. dalla Chiesa, 9, 50136 Firenze FI, Italy
Website: www.otelfirenze.it

TENAX

Tenax nightclub, a staple in Florence's nightlife scene, is famous for its electronic music and live DJ sets. The club has a raw, industrial feel and attracts a diverse crowd of music lovers. With its reputation for hosting renowned DJs and vibrant dance parties, Tenax is a must-visit for electronic music enthusiasts.

Tip: Check out their calendar for special events or guest DJ performances. Arrive late, as the club tends to get going after midnight.

Location: Via Pratese, 46, 50145 Firenze FI, Italy
Website: www.tenax.org

LATE-NIGHT DINING

TRATTORIA 4 LEONI

Trattoria 4 Leoni, located in the historic district of Florence, is a traditional Tuscan restaurant known for its charming ambiance and authentic cuisine. The trattoria, with its rustic decor and warm atmosphere, serves a variety of classic Tuscan dishes, including pasta, grilled meats, and local specialties. It's a perfect spot for a late-night meal in an inviting setting.

Tip: Try their famous 'Fiocchetti di pere in salsa di taleggio e asparagi' (pear and cheese pasta). It's advisable to make a reservation, as the restaurant is popular among both locals and tourists.
Location: Via de' Vellutini, 1r, 50125 Firenze FI, Italy.
Website: www.4leoni.it

OSTERIA SANTO SPIRITO

Osteria Santo Spirito, situated in the lively Santo Spirito square, offers a cozy and relaxed dining experience. This osteria serves delicious Tuscan fare with a modern twist and is known for its generous portions and friendly service. The outdoor seating is perfect for enjoying a late dinner in a vibrant neighborhood.

Tip: Their creamy truffle pasta and grilled steak are highly recommended. Arriving later in the evening often means a more leisurely dining experience.
Location: Piazza Santo Spirito, 16r, 50125 Firenze FI, Italy.
Website: www.facebook.com/osteriasantospiritofirenze/

IL LATINI

Il Latini is a well-known restaurant in Florence, famous for its traditional Tuscan cuisine and bustling atmosphere. Housed in a former wine cellar, the restaurant offers a hearty menu featuring local specialties, homemade pasta, and a variety of meat dishes. The communal seating and lively ambiance make it a fun place for late-night dining.

Tip: Be prepared for a communal dining experience, which is part of the charm of Il Latini. The restaurant also offers an excellent selection of local wines.
Location: Via dei Palchetti, 6R, 50123 Firenze FI, Italy
Website: www.latinifirenze.com/en

GUSTA PIZZA

Gusta Pizza is one of the most popular pizzerias in Florence, offering delicious Neapolitan-style pizzas. Known for its fresh ingredients and wood-fired pizzas, it's a favorite among locals and tourists alike. The casual and lively atmosphere makes it a great choice for a late-night pizza craving.

Tip: The pizzeria can be quite busy, so there might be a wait. However, the authentic and flavorful pizzas are worth it. Try their signature 'Gusta Pizza' with spicy salami.
Location: Via Maggio, 46r, 50125 Firenze FI, Italy
Website: www.facebook.com/GustapizzaFirenze/

NIGHTLIFE AREAS

SANTO SPIRITO SQUARE

Santo Spirito Square, located in the Oltrarno district, is a lively and vibrant area known for its bohemian atmosphere. The square is surrounded by numerous bars, restaurants, and cafes, making it a popular spot for both locals and tourists. The laid-back vibe is perfect for those looking to enjoy a relaxed evening with drinks, good food, and often live music or street performances.

Tip: The area is particularly lively during the summer months when the outdoor seating of the surrounding establishments creates a festive and communal atmosphere.

Location: Piazza Santo Spirito, 50125 Firenze FI, Italy

PIAZZA DELLA SIGNORIA

Piazza della Signoria is one of Florence's most famous squares and a central hub of activity. While known for its historical and architectural significance, the square also boasts a vibrant nightlife scene. The area is filled with upscale bars and cafes, offering a sophisticated setting for an evening out. The illuminated view of the Palazzo Vecchio and surrounding statues adds a magical touch to the night.

Tip: Enjoy an aperitivo at one of the outdoor cafes in the square to soak in the historic atmosphere of Florence at night.

Location: Piazza della Signoria, 50122 Firenze FI, Italy

SANTA CROCE

The Santa Croce area is known for its energetic and youthful vibe, making it a favorite nightlife spot among students and young locals. The neighborhood is filled with a variety of bars, pubs, and clubs that come alive after dark. The lively streets around the Santa Croce church offer a mix of traditional and modern entertainment options.

Tip: This area is great for bar hopping and experiencing the local nightlife scene. It's also a great place to try some local street food for a late-night snack.

Location: Piazza di Santa Croce, 50122 Firenze FI, Italy

VIA DE' BENCI

Via de' Benci is a bustling street in Florence known for its vibrant nightlife. Lined with bars and pubs, this area attracts a lively crowd looking to enjoy a fun night out. The street has a wide range of establishments, from cozy wine bars to lively clubs, catering to diverse tastes and preferences.

Tip: The area gets quite busy, especially on weekends, so it's a good idea to arrive early if you want to secure a spot in your preferred bar or club.

Location: Via de' Benci, 50122 Firenze FI, Italy

SAFETY TIPS

Exploring Florence by night can be an exhilarating experience, but it's important to prioritize your safety to ensure your evening adventures remain pleasant memories. Here are some safety tips to keep in mind:

- **Vigilance is key**: Crowded venues and bustling streets are prime spots for pickpockets. Always be mindful of your personal belongings and consider using anti-theft bags or pouches.
- **Stay in the light**: Stick to well-lit and populated streets, especially if you're venturing out alone. Dark and deserted alleys can be risky, so it's best to avoid them.
- **Trustworthy transport**: Use only reputable taxi companies or verified ride-sharing apps for nighttime travel. It's wise to pre-save the contact details of a reliable taxi service on your phone.
- **Guard your glass**: While enjoying the local nightlife, never leave your drink unattended. Accept beverages only from trusted companions or directly from the bartender.
- **Drink smart**: Consume alcohol in moderation and stay hydrated with water throughout the night. This will help you maintain awareness and make better decisions.
- **Emergency preparedness**: Keep a list of emergency contacts, including local authorities and your embassy, easily accessible. A portable phone charger can be a lifesaver in keeping your device powered up.
- **Document safety**: Carry photocopies of your essential documents, such as your passport, and store the originals in a secure location like a hotel safe.

Remember, the night is yours to enjoy, but staying alert and prepared is the best way to ensure that your nocturnal explorations are safe and enjoyable.

By following these tips and exploring the city by night, you'll be able to experience the magic and charm of the city while staying safe and having an unforgettable time.

ART, HISTORY AND ARCHITECTURE

Florence: The Cradle of the Renaissance and Architectural Splendor

Florence, nestled in the heart of Italy's Tuscany region, is a city that stands as a monumental testament to the Renaissance, a period that reshaped Western art, architecture, and thought. This historic city, with its picturesque streets and squares, has been a focal point of cultural and artistic development since its founding by Julius Caesar in 59 BC.

At the core of Florence's artistic legacy is the Renaissance, a period marked by an extraordinary flourishing of art and knowledge. The city is synonymous with legendary figures like Michelangelo, Leonardo da Vinci, and Botticelli, whose works transformed the artistic landscape. Florence's galleries, most notably the Uffizi and the Accademia, are treasure troves of Renaissance art, housing masterpieces such as Michelangelo's David and Botticelli's The Birth of Venus.

Florence's architectural grandeur is equally impressive. The cityscape is dominated by the Cathedral of Santa Maria del Fiore (the Duomo), with its iconic red-tiled dome engineered by Brunelleschi, a marvel of Renaissance architecture. The Palazzo Vecchio and the Ponte Vecchio bridge, spanning the Arno River, further exemplify the city's architectural heritage, blending beauty with historical significance.

Historically, Florence's rise as a powerful and wealthy city-state during the medieval and Renaissance periods is a story of political intrigue, artistic patronage, and intellectual pursuit. The Medici family, in particular, played a pivotal role in the city's history, their patronage fostering an environment where arts and sciences could thrive.

Architecturally, Florence presents a cohesive blend of medieval and Renaissance styles. The city's layout, with its narrow streets leading to grand piazzas, and its surrounding hills offer panoramic views of this architectural masterpiece.

Florence is not just a city; it's a journey into the heart of human creativity and intellectual achievement. Each building, artwork, and street corner in Florence tells a story of a time when art and science were reborn, making it an essential destination for anyone seeking to experience the essence of the Renaissance.

ART AND CULTURE IN FLORENCE

BARGELLO NATIONAL MUSEUM

The Bargello National Museum, housed in a former palace and prison, is an art museum with a significant collection of Renaissance sculptures. It features works by renowned artists such as Michelangelo, Donatello, and Cellini. The museum's highlights include Donatello's 'David' and 'St. George' and Michelangelo's 'Bacchus.' The architecture of the building itself, with its grand courtyard and medieval halls, is equally impressive. **Tip**: Take your time to explore the lesser-known works in the museum's collection, which are as fascinating as the more famous pieces.

Location: Via del Proconsolo, 4, 50122 Firenze FI, Italy
Website: www.bargellomusei.beniculturali.it/musei/1/bargello/

GUCCI MUSEUM

The Gucci Museum, or Museo Gucci, is dedicated to the iconic Italian fashion brand. Located in the historic Palazzo della Mercanzia, the museum showcases the history and legacy of the House of Gucci through a collection of vintage and contemporary pieces, including clothing, accessories, and artwork. The museum offers a unique insight into the world of fashion and design. **Tip**: Don't miss the contemporary art installations within the museum, which often reflect the interplay between fashion and art.

Location: P.za della Signoria, 10, 50122 Firenze FI, Italy
Website: https://guccipalazzo.gucci.com/#/en/

MUSEUM OF SAN MARCO

The Museum of San Marco, housed in a historic Dominican convent, is renowned for its collection of Renaissance art, particularly the works of Fra Angelico. The museum's highlights include a series of frescoes by Fra Angelico located in the monks' cells, the Last Supper in the refectory, and a library designed by Michelozzo. It offers a serene and contemplative experience, highlighting the spiritual and artistic life of the 15th-century monks.

Tip: Don't miss the chance to see the famous 'Annunciation' fresco by Fra Angelico. The museum is usually less crowded, allowing for a more intimate viewing experience.
Location: Piazza San Marco, 3, 50121 Firenze FI, Italy
Website: www.feelflorence.it/en/node/12264

LEONARDO DA VINCI MUSEUM

The Leonardo da Vinci Museum is dedicated to the genius of Leonardo, showcasing interactive exhibits of his inventions, drawings, and scientific studies. The museum offers a hands-on experience, particularly appealing to children and adults alike, with working models of Leonardo's machines. It's a fascinating insight into the mind of one of history's greatest inventors and artists.

Tip: The museum is relatively small and can be explored in about an hour, making it a perfect educational break while exploring the city.
Location: Via dei Servi, 66/R, 50122 Firenze FI, Italy
Website: www.leonardointeractivemuseum.com/en/

TEATRO DELLA PERGOLA

Teatro della Pergola, a jewel in the crown of Florence's cultural scene, is an opera house steeped in history and artistic tradition. Dating back to the 17th century, it holds the distinction of being one of Italy's oldest theatres. Famous for its opulent interior, adorned with rich decorations and boasting exceptional acoustics, the theatre has witnessed the premieres of many significant operas and plays, playing a pivotal role in the history of Italian theatre. The horseshoe-shaped auditorium and the historic stage provide an immersive experience into the world of classical theatre and opera. Attending a performance at Teatro della Pergola is not just an evening out; it's a journey through time, offering a glimpse into the grandeur of Italian cultural heritage.

Tip: To fully embrace the theatre's atmosphere, consider attending one of the classical opera or drama performances. The theatre's program is diverse, catering to a wide range of tastes. Booking tickets in advance is recommended, especially for popular shows. For non-Italian speakers, experiencing the performance transcends the language barrier, as the theatre's historic ambiance and the quality of productions speak a universal language of art.

Location: Via della Pergola, 12/32, 50121 Firenze FI, Italy
Website: www.teatrodellatoscana.it/it/teatri/teatro-della-pergola

FLORENCE OPERA HOUSE

The Florence Opera House, or Opera di Firenze, represents a perfect blend of contemporary architecture and cultural heritage in the heart of Florence. This modern marvel is celebrated for its exceptional acoustics and state-of-the-art facilities, making it a premier venue for the performing arts. The opera house's diverse program includes world-class opera, ballet, and classical music concerts, attracting both local and international audiences. The building itself, with its sleek, innovative design, stands in contrast to the historical backdrop of the city, offering a unique artistic and architectural experience. Inside, the spacious auditorium and cutting-edge stage technology provide an immersive and unforgettable performance experience. For lovers of the performing arts, a visit to the Florence Opera House is an opportunity to witness the vibrant contemporary cultural scene of Florence.

Tip: Even if your schedule doesn't allow for attending a performance, the opera house offers guided tours, providing an insight into its architectural splendor and history. These tours are a fantastic way to appreciate the venue's contribution to the arts and to understand the intricacies of modern theatre design. Booking tickets for performances or tours in advance is highly recommended.

Location: Piazza Vittorio Gui, 1, 50144 Firenze FI, Italy
Website: www.maggiofiorentino.com

HISTORICAL AND ARCHITECTURAL LANDMARKS IN FLORENCE

BAPTISTERY OF ST. JOHN

The Baptistery of St. John is one of Florence's oldest buildings, known for its remarkable architecture and the striking bronze doors, including the famous Gates of Paradise by Lorenzo Ghiberti. The octagonal structure is a masterpiece of Florentine Romanesque architecture. Inside, visitors can admire the beautiful mosaics covering the dome and the marble flooring.

Tip: While the exterior is impressive, don't miss the interior for its stunning mosaics. Early morning is the best time to visit to avoid crowds.

Location: Piazza San Giovanni, 50122 Firenze FI, Italy
Website: https://duomo.firenze.it/en/discover/baptistry

FORTEZZA DA BASSO

Fortezza da Basso, a fortress built in the mid-16th century, is a prominent example of Renaissance military architecture. Originally designed by Antonio da Sangallo the Younger for the Medici, it now serves as a venue for conferences, exhibitions, and cultural events. The fortress combines historical significance with a role in contemporary events, representing the dynamic nature of Florence.

Tip: Check the events schedule before visiting; the fortress often hosts interesting exhibitions and fairs that can be an added bonus to your visit.

Location: V.le Filippo Strozzi, 1, 50129 Firenze FI, Italy
Website: www.firenzefiera.it/en

ORSANMICHELE CHURCH

Orsanmichele Church is a remarkable historical and architectural landmark in Florence, showcasing a blend of religious significance and artistic splendor. Originally constructed as a grain market in the 14th century, it was transformed into a church, embodying the distinctive Gothic style of the era. The church's exterior is adorned with exquisite sculptures by renowned artists such as Donatello, Ghiberti, and Verrocchio, each contributing to its ornate façade. Inside, the church houses the revered Tabernacle of the Madonna delle Grazie, an outstanding example of Florentine Gothic art. Orsanmichele's interior is a testament to the artistic mastery of the time, with artworks that captivate visitors. This church is not just a place of worship but also a gallery of medieval art and architecture.

Tip: For a more comprehensive experience, visit on a Monday to access the upper floor and terrace. This vantage point offers an up-close view of the external sculptures and panoramic views of Florence, providing a unique perspective on the city's historic landscape.

Location: Via dell'Arte della Lana, 50123 Firenze FI, Italy.
Website: www.feelflorence.it/en/node/12154

PIAZZA DELLA REPUBBLICA

Piazza della Repubblica stands at the heart of Florence as a symbol of the city's evolution from ancient times to the present day. This historic square marks the site of the ancient Roman forum, the birthplace of Florence. Over the centuries, it has witnessed significant transformations, evolving from a medieval market to a grandiose space of the Risanamento, a period of urban renewal in Florence. Today, the square is characterized by its imposing arch, the Arcone, and a vibrant carousel that adds a touch of whimsy. Piazza della Repubblica is surrounded by elegant buildings and iconic cafes that have been frequented by writers and artists over the years. This lively square is a melting pot of history, culture, and modern Florentine life, making it a popular gathering place for both locals and tourists. The blend of architectural styles around the square tells the story of Florence's dynamic history and its enduring charm.

Tip: Take a moment to enjoy a coffee or aperitivo at one of the historic cafes around the square. Cafes like Caffè Gilli and Paszkowski offer a perfect vantage point to appreciate the square's vibrant atmosphere and watch the world go by. The square is also an excellent spot for photography, capturing the essence of Florence's lively urban scene.

Location: Piazza della Repubblica, 50123 Firenze FI, Italy.
Website: www.visittuscany.com/en/attractions/piazza-della-repubblica-in-florence/

SANTA MARIA NOVELLA CHURCH

The Church of Santa Maria Novella is a magnificent cornerstone of Florence's architectural and artistic heritage. This beautiful church, standing near the city's main train station, is a stunning blend of Gothic and Renaissance styles. Its façade, masterfully designed by Leon Battista Alberti, is a landmark of Renaissance architecture, characterized by harmonious proportions and elegant use of geometric forms. The interior of the church is a treasure trove of art, featuring masterpieces such as Masaccio's 'Trinity,' a pivotal work in the development of perspective in art, and Ghirlandaio's frescoes, which are renowned for their vivid detail and historical significance. The Tornabuoni Chapel and the Spanish Chapel within the church are also highlights, containing frescoes that depict scenes of religious and historical importance. Each corner of Santa Maria Novella offers insights into the rich cultural and spiritual life of Florence during the Renaissance.

Tip: To fully experience the church's artistic wealth, don't miss the cloisters and the adjacent museum, where you can find additional art pieces and relics. These areas offer a quieter and more contemplative atmosphere, allowing visitors to appreciate the church's art and history away from the crowds. The museum also provides context to the artworks and the church's historical significance in Florence.

Location: P.za di Santa Maria Novella, 18, 50123 Firenze FI, Italy
Website: www.smn.it/en/

DAY TRIPS FROM FLORENCE

FIESOLE

Just a short bus ride from Florence, Fiesole offers a tranquil escape with stunning views of Florence and the Tuscan countryside. This charming hilltop town is rich in history, with Etruscan and Roman ruins, including an ancient Roman amphitheater that's still in use today. The town also boasts beautiful villas, gardens, and several museums. **Travel Time**: Approximately 8 km from Florence, around 20-30 minutes by bus.

Tip: Visit the Archaeological Museum and Area, which includes the Roman Theater, Thermal Baths, and the Etruscan Temple. The panoramic views from the Franciscan Missionary Museum are also a must-see.

Website: www.visittuscany.com/en/ideas/things-to-do-and-see-in-fiesole/

SIENA

Siena, known for its medieval streets and the famous Palio horse race, is one of the most beautiful cities in Tuscany. The historic center, a UNESCO World Heritage site, is home to the magnificent Siena Cathedral and the Piazza del Campo, one of Europe's greatest medieval squares. The city's museums, art, and architecture are a testament to its rich history and cultural heritage. **Travel Time**: Approximately 70 km from Florence, around 1.5 hours by bus or train.

Tip: Try to visit the Torre del Mangia for a breathtaking view of the city and the surrounding countryside. The climb is challenging but worth the effort.

Website: www.visitsienaofficial.it/en/

SAN GIMIGNANO

San Gimignano, known as the Town of Fine Towers, is famous for its well-preserved medieval architecture and tower houses. The town's skyline is unmistakable and offers a glimpse into what many medieval Tuscan towns once looked like. The UNESCO World Heritage site is also known for its art, history, and the Vernaccia di San Gimignano wine.

Travel Time: Approximately 60 km from Florence, around 1.5 hours by bus or car.

Tip: Don't miss a wine tasting of the Vernaccia di San Gimignano, the region's famed white wine. The town can get crowded, so an early start is advisable for a more peaceful experience.

Website: www.sangimignano.com/en/

PISA

Pisa is world-famous for its iconic Leaning Tower, but the city offers much more. Located in Pisa's Piazza dei Miracoli, the tower is part of a complex that also includes the beautiful Pisa Cathedral and Baptistery. The city itself has a vibrant street life and a wealth of historical buildings and bridges along the Arno River.

Travel Time: Approximately 85 km from Florence, around 1 hour by train.

Tip: Besides visiting the tower, take time to explore the historic center of Pisa and enjoy a walk along the river.
Climbing the tower requires a timed-entry ticket, which is best booked in advance.

Website: www.turismo.pisa.it/en

CHIANTI WINE REGION

The Chianti region, nestled between Florence and Siena, is renowned for its wine production and stunning landscapes. A trip to Chianti offers the opportunity to visit vineyards and wineries, taste world-class Chianti wines, and enjoy the region's picturesque rolling hills, olive groves, and charming medieval villages.

Travel Time: Varies within the region, but generally about 30 to 60 minutes by car from Florence.

Tip: Consider booking a guided wine tour for a hassle-free experience that often includes transportation and visits to multiple wineries with tastings and sometimes local food pairings.

Website: www.visitchianti.net/?lang=en

LUCCA

Lucca is a charming Tuscan city known for its well-preserved Renaissance walls that encircle the historic old town. The city's streets are filled with quaint shops, cafes, and rich history, including beautiful churches and towers. Lucca is also famous for its vibrant cultural life and hosts several festivals throughout the year.

Travel Time: Approximately 80 km from Florence, around 1.5 hours by train or bus.

Tip: Rent a bike to ride atop the city walls for a unique perspective of Lucca. The walls provide a wide, tree-lined path that's perfect for cycling or a leisurely walk.

Website: www.turismo.lucca.it/en

VAL D'ORCIA

Val d'Orcia, a UNESCO World Heritage site, is renowned for its stunning landscapes that have inspired many Renaissance painters. This region in Tuscany offers picturesque rolling hills, cypress-lined roads, medieval castles, and charming villages like Pienza and Montalcino.

It's also known for its superb wines and pecorino cheese.

Travel Time: Approximately 120 km from Florence, around 2 hours by car.

Tip: The area is ideal for scenic drives and wine tasting. Visiting the historic town of Pienza for its Renaissance architecture and cheese shops is highly recommended.

Website: www.parcodellavaldorcia.com

CINQUE TERRE

The Cinque Terre is a string of five colorful fishing villages perched on the rugged Italian Riviera coastline. Linked by walking paths, these villages are known for their stunning views, vibrant houses, and crystal-clear waters. A visit to Cinque Terre offers a chance to enjoy beautiful hikes, delicious seafood, and a relaxed coastal atmosphere.

Travel Time: Approximately 170 km from Florence, around 2.5 hours by train or car.

Tip: Consider purchasing the Cinque Terre Card, which offers unlimited train travel between the villages and access to the hiking trails.

Website: www.cinqueterre.it/en/

AREZZO

Arezzo, an enchanting city in eastern Tuscany, is known for its medieval architecture, frescoes by Piero della Francesca in the Basilica di San Francesco, and its Antiques Fair held in the Piazza Grande. The city has a rich history and a vibrant cultural scene, making it a delightful destination for those interested in art, antiques, and architecture.

Travel Time: Approximately 80 km from Florence, around 1 hour by train.

Tip: The first weekend of each month hosts the famous Antiques Fair, a must-visit for collectors and enthusiasts.

Travel Time from San Sebastian: Approximately 40 minutes by car or 1 hour by public transport.

Website: www.comune.arezzo.it

MONTEPULCIANO

Montepulciano is a medieval and Renaissance hill town in southern Tuscany, famous for its Noble wine. The town is encircled by walls and fortifications and offers stunning views of the Tuscan countryside. Visitors can enjoy its beautiful Renaissance buildings, charming streets, and numerous wine cellars offering tastings of Montepulciano wine.

Travel Time: Approximately 120 km from Florence, around 1.5 hours by car.

Tip: Take a wine tour to explore the local vineyards and enjoy the Vino Nobile di Montepulciano, one of Italy's most prestigious wines.

Website: www.visittuscany.com/en/towns-and-villages/montepulciano/

END NOTE

As we conclude this guide to Florence, it becomes clear that this city is not merely a destination; it's a living museum of art, history, and culture. Florence, cradled in the heart of Tuscany, beckons you to delve into its rich tapestry, from the majestic Duomo to the timeless streets of the historic center. This city is a mosaic of experiences, each nook echoing with tales of the Renaissance, and every cobblestone street whispering stories of past and present.

Florence's narrative is a beautiful blend of its glorious past and vibrant present. The artistic legacy of Michelangelo and Da Vinci coexists with the contemporary rhythms of modern Italian life. Its architecture, a stunning array of Renaissance splendor and urban charm, mirrors Florence's reverence for its historical roots and its embrace of the present.

The culinary delights of Florence are as captivating as its art. From quaint trattorias serving traditional Tuscan fare to elegant restaurants offering innovative cuisine, the city entices the palate. Its gastronomy celebrates the richness of Italian flavors, nurtured by the region's bountiful produce and culinary heritage.

Departing from Florence, you take with you more than just memories; you carry a piece of its soul. The beauty of the Arno River, the splendor of its art, the aroma of fresh Tuscan cuisine, and the warmth of its people stay with you. You leave behind the Renaissance masterpieces, the serene Boboli Gardens, and the lively piazzas, but with the knowledge that Florence is a city to revisit, to explore anew.

Florence is a testament to the enduring spirit and hospitality of its inhabitants. It's a city that celebrates art and life in all its forms, a place where nature's beauty and human creativity exist in perfect harmony. Florence is a destination for all, a city that reveals its wonders and familiar joys with each visit.

As this guide ends, remember that Florence is not just the culmination of a journey; it's an ongoing exploration. It's a city that stays in your heart, inviting you to return, to rediscover, and to fall in love with it again and again. Florence awaits your next visit with open arms and a promise: the magic of this city is timeless, and each return will be as enchanting as the first.

Embark on your journey through this city of art, and let the enduring allure of Florence inspire you, today and forever.

EXTRA RESOURCES

Florence maps

Florence General Map

Florence Tourist Map

Florence City Center Map

Florence Travel Map

Florence Public Transport Map

Florence Bike Map

Region Tourist Routes

Florence card

Official Tourism Site of Florence

Official Tourism Site of Tuscany

TRAVEL

PLACES TO SEE:

LOCAL FOOD TO TRY:

DAY 1	DAY 2	DAY 3

DAY 4	DAY 5	DAY 6

NOTES

PLANNER

⭐⭐⭐⭐⭐

Loved Your Journey With Our Guide?
Your feedback makes a world of difference! If our guide helped you explore or enjoy your destination, we would be thrilled if you could take a moment to leave us a 5-star review on our product page.

Simply click the link or go to any of our product pages on your preferred retailer website and **share your recommendations.**
https://www.amazon.com/stores/Tailored-Travel-Guides/author/B0C4TV5TZX

Scan the QR Code to share your recommendations

Join our Tailored Travel Guides Network
for more benefits by accessing this link:
https://mailchi.mp/d151cba349e8/ttgnetwork
Or by scanning the QR code

Thank you for chosing Tailored Travel Guides!

Discover Your Journey

UNLOCK A WORLD OF UNFORGETTABLE EXPERIENCES WITH TAILORED TRAVEL GUIDES!

As your go-to source for personalized and meticulously crafted travel guides, we ensure that every adventure is uniquely yours. Our team of dedicated travel experts and local insiders design each guide with your preferences, interests, and travel style in mind, providing you with the ultimate customized travel experience.

Embark on your next journey with confidence, knowing that Tailored Travel Guides has got you covered. To explore more exceptional destinations and discover a treasure trove of additional guides, visit www.tailoredtravelguides.com. or our collection available on:

Amazon at this link: www.amazon.com/stores/Tailored-Travel-Guides/author/B0C4TV5TZX or
on **Google Play**, at this link:
https://play.google.com/store/books/author?id=Tailored+Travel+Guides
on **Etsy**, at this link: https://tailoredtravelguides.etsy.com

Happy travels, and here's to a lifetime of remarkable memories!

ALSO IN THE SERIES

Turin	Bologna
Rome	Milan
Genoa	Venice
Verona	Florence
Naples	Palermo

CHECK OUT THE SPAIN UNVEILED SERIES

Malaga

Valencia

Cordoba

Toledo

Madrid

Granada

Barcelona

Seville

Bilbao

San Sebastian

Tenerife

CHECK OUT THE FRANCE UNVEILED SERIES

Marseille

Nantes

Toulouse

Nice

Paris

Lille

Lyon

Montpellier

Bordeaux

Strasbourg

Made in the USA
Las Vegas, NV
08 June 2024